How do living things find food?

Bobbie Kalman

🌳 **Crabtree Publishing Company**

www.crabtreebooks.com

Introducing Living Things

Created by Bobbie Kalman

Dedicated by Crystal Sikkens
For my new nephew, Ethan John Snippe, with love

**Author and
Editor-in-Chief**
Bobbie Kalman

Editor
Kathy Middleton

Proofreader
Crystal Sikkens

Design
Bobbie Kalman
Katherine Berti

**Production coordinator
and Prepress technician**
Katherine Berti

Photo research
Bobbie Kalman

Illustrations
Barbara Bedell: pages 5, 24
Katherine Berti: page 6
Bonna Rouse: page 12

Photographs
BigStockPhoto: page 10
iStockPhoto.com: page 14 (top)
Photos.com: pages 6, 24 (herbivores)
Other photographs by Shutterstock

Library and Archives Canada Cataloguing in Publication

Kalman, Bobbie, 1947-
    How do living things find food? / Bobbie Kalman.

(Introducing living things)
Includes index.
Issued also in an electronic format.
ISBN 978-0-7787-3234-1 (bound).--ISBN 978-0-7787-3258-7 (pbk.)

    1. Animals--Food--Juvenile literature. 2. Photosynthesis--Juvenile
literature. 3. Food chains (Ecology)--Juvenile literature.
I. Title. II. Series.

QL756.5.K343 2011   j591.5'3   C2010-902745-0

Library of Congress Cataloging-in-Publication Data

Kalman, Bobbie.
  How do living things find food? / Bobbie Kalman.
    p. cm. -- (Introducing living things)
  Includes index.
  ISBN 978-0-7787-3258-7 (pbk. : alk. paper) -- ISBN 978-0-7787-3234-1
(reinforced library binding : alk. paper) -- ISBN 978-1-4271-9490-9
(electronic (pdf))
  1. Animals--Food--Juvenile literature. 2. Photosynthesis--Juvenile
literature. 3. Food chains (Ecology)--Juvenile literature. I. Title. II. Series.

QL756.5.K353 2011
591.5'3--dc22
                                              2010016401

Crabtree Publishing Company

www.crabtreebooks.com   1-800-387-7650

Printed in China/082010/AP20100512

**Published in Canada
Crabtree Publishing**
616 Welland Ave.
St. Catharines, Ontario
L2M 5V6

**Published in the United States
Crabtree Publishing**
PMB 59051
350 Fifth Avenue, 59th Floor
New York, New York 10118

**Published in the United Kingdom
Crabtree Publishing**
Maritime House
Basin Road North, Hove
BN41 1WR

**Published in Australia
Crabtree Publishing**
386 Mt. Alexander Rd.
Ascot Vale (Melbourne)
VIC 3032

Contents

Food energy

What is a **living thing**? Plants are living things. Animals are living things. People are living things. Living things grow and change. To stay alive, living things need air, water, and food. Food gives living things the **energy** they need. Living things need energy to move and grow. They cannot do anything without energy.

We could not stay alive for very long without food. We need different kinds of food.

Energy comes from the sun. Plants catch the sun's energy and use it to make food. They make food from sunlight, air, and water. Making food using sunlight is called **photosynthesis**.

Photosynthesis

leaves

sunlight

air

soil

roots

water

The roots of plants take in water from the soil. The leaves of plants take in air and sunlight. Food is made in the leaves of plants.

Plant eaters

The energy of sunlight is stored in plants. When animals or people eat plants, they get the energy of the sun, too. The sun's energy is passed along to the plant eaters. Animals that eat mainly plants are called **herbivores**.

This groundhog has found some spring flowers to eat.

Different herbivores eat different parts of plants. Some eat grasses and leaves. Some eat fruit, nuts, seeds, flowers, and even wood. Some drink **nectar**. Nectar is a sweet liquid found in flowers.

This mouse found grass seeds to eat.

Squirrels like nuts, seeds, and fruit.

This bee is drinking nectar from a flower.

Looking for food

This pony is a grazer. It has the right kind of teeth and stomach for eating grasses.

Many herbivores are **grazers**. Grazers eat grass and other plants that grow close to the ground. Horses are grazers. They have special stomachs that can break down the grasses they eat. Some herbivores are **browsers**. Browsers eat the leaves of bushes and trees.

There are grasses in oceans, too. Manatees are big ocean grazers. Their mouths are like vacuum cleaners. They can quickly "clean" an area of sea grasses.

8

Caterpillars eat a lot of leaves before they become butterflies!

Giraffes are browsers with long necks. They can reach the leaves of tall trees.

Butterflies drink flower nectar. A butterfly has a **proboscis** that can reach inside flowers to suck up the nectar. The proboscis is like a straw.

Many herbivores, such as these lemurs, like to eat fruit.

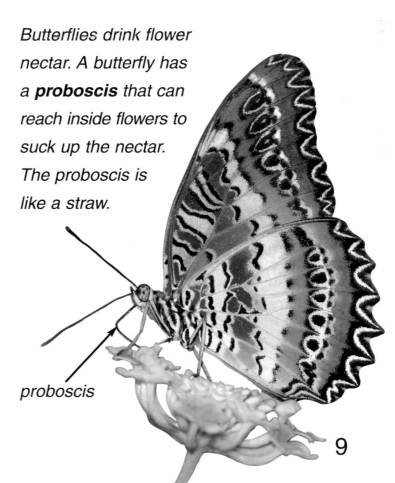

proboscis

Carnivores eat meat

Animals that eat other animals are called **carnivores**. "Carnivore" means "meat eater." Most carnivores are **predators**. Predators hunt the animals they eat. The animals that predators hunt are called **prey**.

Wolves are predators that hunt in groups called packs.
This wolf pack has hunted a deer.

10

Cats, such as lions, tigers, and leopards, are big carnivores. They have sharp teeth called **canines** for grabbing their prey. The **ridges** on the roof of a cat's mouth help hold its prey.

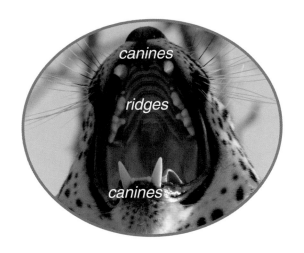

This leopard is dragging its prey up into a tree so other carnivores will not steal it.

Air, land, and water

Predators hunt in the air, on land, and in water. Some birds use their beaks for catching prey. Other birds have sharp **talons**, or claws, for grabbing their prey.

This hawk has grabbed a fish out of water with its talons.

Many fish are carnivores. This great white shark is hunting a seal in water. It has sharp teeth for catching fish, seals, dolphins, and other ocean animals.

This heron has found a rat to eat. It holds the rat in its long beak.

Alligators catch fish in water. On land, they can hunt animals as big as deer. They can run fast.

Some snakes use **venom**, or poison, to stop their prey from moving.

Insect eaters

This sundew plant has trapped an insect with its sticky leaves.

Some carnivores look for **insects** to eat. Insects are small animals with six legs. Birds, frogs, fish, and many other animals eat insects. Animals that eat mainly insects are called **insectivores**. Some plants, such as sundews, also eat insects!

Spiders eat flies, moths, and other insects. This jumping spider has jumped on a fly to eat.

Many spiders weave webs for catching their prey.

This chameleon shot out its long, sticky tongue to catch a fly. Frogs also catch insects this way.

claws

Anteaters use their sharp claws to dig up ant nests. They eat other insects, too. Their long, sticky tongues grab the insects.

(right) Praying mantises pretend to be leaves, branches, and flowers so their prey will not see them. What does this mantis look like?

15

What are omnivores?

Omnivores are animals that eat both plants and other animals. Their bodies can live on one or both kinds of foods. Skunks, raccoons, chipmunks, foxes, and many bears are omnivores.

Most birds are omnivores. This blue jay eats nuts, seeds, and other plant foods, but it also eats insects and worms.

Chipmunks eat any food they find. They stuff their cheeks with food.

16

Black bears eat mainly plants, but they also eat insects, fish, and even animals as big as deer or moose. This baby bear may find nuts or insects to eat in this tree.

grub

Skunks eat plants, but they also eat insects, frogs, birds, and eggs. They love grubs!

Opossums eat any foods they find— even garbage.

Foxes are carnivores that will eat plants if they cannot find animals to hunt.

Food chains

Energy comes from the sun and is used by plants to make food. The sun's energy is passed along in **food chains**. The food chain on the next page is made up of a sunflower, a squirrel, and a fox. They all have the sun's energy inside them.

sun
energy

The sunflower
makes food.
The sun's energy
is passed along.

The squirrel eats sunflower
seeds. The sun's energy is
passed along to the squirrel.

A fox eats the squirrel. The sun's
energy is passed along to the fox.

19

Nature's cleaners

When living things die, they still have energy and **nutrients** in their bodies. Nutrients are the parts of food that keep our bodies healthy. Predators hunt animals, eat some of the meat, and then leave the rest behind. Other animals get the nutrients from the leftovers. Animals that eat the leftovers of dead animals are called **scavengers**.

Eagles are both predators and scavengers. This eagle has found a dead fox to eat. It is a scavenger when it eats an animal it did not hunt. Scavengers help clean Earth.

Earthworms eat dead plants and also dig tunnels. Air comes into the soil through the tunnels. Air makes the soil better.

This ant has found a dead fly to eat. It is cleaning the forest when it eats dead animals.

Mushrooms are not plants. They are living things called **fungi**. Fungi are the only cleaners that can break down dead trees. Mushrooms also clean the soil.

Food for people

How do people find food? Most people buy food in **supermarkets**. Farmers grow vegetables and fruits and raise animals, such as chickens. The foods are then taken to supermarkets in trucks.

The boy below is going to eat a pizza. Pizza is made with flour and tomatoes, which come from plants. It also has cheese and meat, which come from animals.

Some people do not eat meat, but most people eat every kind of food. They eat fruits, vegetables, eggs, meat, cheese, fish, and mushrooms. Name ten kinds of foods in the picture below that you eat.

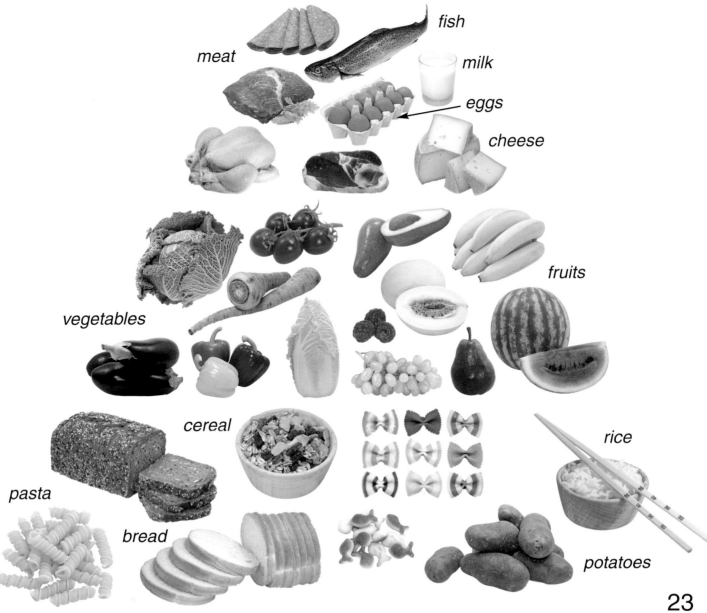

fish

meat

milk

eggs

cheese

fruits

vegetables

cereal

rice

pasta

bread

potatoes

Words to know and Index

carnivores
pages 10–15, 17

food chains
pages 18–19

herbivores
pages 6–9

insectivores
pages 14–15

omnivores
pages 16–17

people
pages 4, 6,
22–23

plants
pages 4, 5,
6–7, 8, 14, 16,
17, 18, 21, 22

Other index words

predators
pages 10,
12, 20

prey
pages 10, 11,
12, 13, 14, 15

scavengers
page 20